Kristin Tillotson

Retro Housewife

A Salute to the
Suburban Superwoman

PORTLAND, OREGON

Cover Design: Wade Daughtry, Collectors Press, Inc.
Book Design: Jeff Birndorf, endesign
Editors: Jennifer Weaver-Neist and Bernadette Baker

Library of Congress Cataloging-in-Publication Data

Tillotson, Kristin, 1959-
    Retro housewife : a salute to the suburban superwoman / by Kristin
Tillotson.-- 1st American ed.
        p. cm. -- (Retro series)
    ISBN 1-888054-92-1 (hardcover : alk. paper)
 1. Home economics. I. Title. II. Series.
    TX145.M295 2004
    640--dc22
                                        2003027517

Printed in Singapore

9 8 7 6 5 4 3 2 1

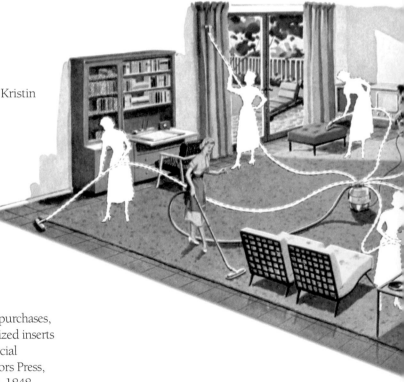

Collectors Press books are available at special discounts for bulk purchases,
premiums, and promotions. Special editions, including personalized inserts
or covers, and corporate logos, can be printed in quantity for special
purposes. For further information contact: Special Sales, Collectors Press,
Inc., P.O. Box 230986, Portland, OR 97281. Toll free: 1-800-423-1848.

For a free catalog write: Collectors Press, Inc., P.O. Box 230986, Portland,
OR 97281. Toll free: 1-800-423-1848 or visit our website at:
www.collectorspress.com.

Contents

I love to wear my mother's old floral-print apron when I'm working in my kitchen. It's faded, threadbare, peppered with antique burn marks and Crisco spots that no amount of scrubbing can remove. Now that I'm all grown up with a job and home of my own, I can certainly afford to buy a brand new apron made of stain-resistant, high-tech fabric. But I prefer my mom's because, when I slip it on, I slip back in time.

Like the majority of American baby boomers' mothers, mine was a housewife — a label that has ridden a roller coaster of connotation over the last 50 years. In the mid-20th century, being a stay-at-home mom was considered the pinnacle of success. When feminism and the sexual revolution of the 1960s came along, being a housewife was shameful, a prison sentence for timid underachievers. Over the next two decades, the concept of a woman's fulfillment — keeping a tidy home, raising polite children, and tending to her husband's comfort — began to seem as dated as Victorian values.

Then, around the turn of the new millennium, something happened. In no way did women with careers, independence, and expertise in multi-tasking fancy returning to the limitations of the old days. But the well-documented stresses involved with "having it all" were giving rise to a wistful longing for simpler lives.

The trend once called cocooning was renamed "nesting" and continued to grow. So did, what some pundits called, "the domestic-bliss industry." Old-style home cooking was once again in vogue, a guilty pleasure loaded with carbohydrates, fat, and salt. The comforting accoutrements of the 1950s, such as Fiesta dinnerware and brightly colored aluminum tumblers, began appearing on store shelves once again. Hip magazines started running articles on the joys of housework, lending it such qualities as therapeutic, self-esteem building, even thrilling. Martha Stewart, the all-time queen of domestic goddesses, began to experience the kind of runaway popularity formerly reserved for pop idols.

Of course, emulating Martha didn't exactly make life simpler. Nor did the latter-day housewife float through her days on a carefree cloud of whipped pie topping. She did, however, live a life in which her role was sharply defined, the borders of her territory clearly marked. She hovered around her bread-winning man and their children, making their meals and cleaning up after them as if that was what she'd been put on earth to do. As the original "do-it-yourselfer," she was also frugal,

6

keeping up appearances — her own and her home's — on a shoestring budget. From the turbulence of World War II through the optimism-drenched 1950s, a woman's place was indeed in the home.

Retro Housewife is a rose-tinted look back at those times, a window into a world that existed in Life magazine layouts, advertisements for household appliances, and, to a certain degree, many real-life suburban homes. Daily life was less complicated, everything moved more slowly, and people were happier — or at least seemed that way.

During the workforce shortages brought on by World War II, women marched out of their kitchens and into their husbands' paycheck-earning places, symbolized by Rosie the Riveter and her "We Can Do It!" slogan. An astounding 60.2 percent of women worked outside the home during the war, a number nearly approaching modern census figures.

They sure got sent back home in a hurry. By 1948, the number of American women aged 16 and older in the labor force had shrunk to less than 33 percent. In the pre-dawn of the Eisenhower era, the country was poised to live out the most idealized family-values chapter of the 20th century.

Women married at an average age of 20 in 1950, men at 23. Divorce was rare and hard to obtain (the rate in 1950 was 2.5 percent, compared with nearly 50 percent today). Marriage counseling was a new-fangled notion. My goodness, if your family was well fed and lived in a flawlessly painted rambler surrounded by a weed-free, mowed and edged lawn, why would you need therapy?

Obesity was also rare, despite a much more fatty diet, because the retro housewife expended so many calories on her daily routine, toting bags from the neighborhood shops home on foot and being active from dawn till dusk.

Median family incomes doubled during the boom years of the 1950s, an impossible dream for most families today. Compared to the penny-pinching, all-for-one patriotism of the 1940s, the 1950s — a period during which spending on advertising quadrupled — ushered in a culture of commercialism, with status more directly connected to buying power. Women were the primary consumers, and thus the top target of product promotions.

Ads encouraged the retro housewife to have a personal relationship with her appliances, which were often given miraculous qualities; the word "magic" was applied to everything from scrubbing pads to tomato sauce to hand lotion. Household products were given cute personifications like Borden's Elsie the Cow. The poetry of Sylvia Plath both described and mocked this trend with such lines as "When I am quiet at my cooking, I feel it looking" and "The smile of iceboxes annihilates me. / Such blue currents in the veins of my loved one! / I hear her great heart purr."

That attitude became more strident and wide-spread after the 1963 publication of Betty Friedan's *The Feminine Mystique* — the book that blew housewives' minds from the Hamptons to the boondocks by suggesting they could ask for more than secondary status. Amid the counterculture revolution and the release of the birth-control pill, women's options were suddenly all over the map. Housewives were no longer positive role models, but doormats at worst, martyrs at best.

But to the retro housewife, the home was less a spick-and-span prison cell than an ongoing project that provided her with a deep sense of purpose and identity. Her castle may have been a one-story rambler, but in a time when marriage and babies were considered the pinnacle of every woman's personal success, it still made her feel like a queen. She didn't consider herself a robotic Stepford Wife but a crucial cog in the wheel of American prosperity.

Television and the movies — which were also experiencing their "golden" ages — influenced the tenor of the times in a more sweeping, universal way than they do today. Everyone loved Lucy and Ethel, whose lives, for all their adventures stomping grapes and messing up candy assembly lines, were still focused on home and family. As for titillation, Marilyn Monroe's dress-blowing stint over the grate in *The Seven-Year Itch* and the surf-pounding make-out session between Burt Lancaster and Deborah Kerr in *From Here To Eternity* were just about as risqué as the modest housewife could handle.

The deeply etched gender roles that gave structure and order to the running of the household also governed the retro housewife's appearance. By today's standards, her style dilemma seems insurmountable: dress modestly, yet also like a vixen able to erase all of hubby's workaday woes with one G-rated come-hither greeting at the door. Look like an all-American mother *and* an all-American bombshell — half June Cleaver, half Marilyn.

Lucky thing she had plenty of guidance from McCall's and the movies. To appear both sexy and chaste, the proper wife and mommy needed to pay attention to the details — a dramatic sweep with the Max Factor brow pencil, sturdily built shoes that happened to feature a peek-a-boo open toe and 3-inch heels, strategically cut angora sweater sets, a form-fitting pencil skirt in a ladylike pastel hue, and, of course, the finishing touch: a demure handbag.

As hairstyles evolved from the curls and up-dos of the 1940s to the ponytails, peroxide, and beehives of the 1950s, her closet held corresponding supplies of crinoline and chiffon, gingham and polka dots. No sweat pants and T-shirts for her. Casual wear was a pair of smart capri pants, striped blouse, and matching headband. At home, however, when it was time to get down to work, her uniform was the housedress, which *The Ladies' Home Journal Art of Homemaking* suggested should be "wide enough for action, but not so wide it will get in your way or make you trip on stairs or a ladder…" Even so, a housedress could achieve nipped-in, hourglass definition when corralled by a crisp apron.

Studies claim that the average woman's waistline has increased over the past 50 years from a mere 23 inches to 32. Perhaps those wickedly constricting foundation garments of the past helped a bit in the illusion department. Most every child of the 1950s can clearly recall Mom's groan from the bedroom as she slipped out of her pre-Lycra girdle. Between that, a brassiere strong enough to buoy Mount Rushmore, stockings that had to be held up with garter belts, and a few layers of lace-trimmed slips for extra protection, she had to get herself in and out of more daily trappings than a four-star general.

Like everything else about the retro housewife, her ability to achieve simultaneous perfection in grooming and home maintenance is best perceived through the gauze filter of nostalgia. But there's a reason that modern fashion designers return with regularity to her "look" — it's a classic, just like her.

We can't go back (even if we wanted to). But *Retro Housewife* can take us there, if only for a little while.

Now, dears, it's time to come along with Mother on a trip down memory lane — that is, if you've finished your homework, washed your hands, and put your bike away.

Women of today think they're under a lot of pressure. What a hill of beans, the housewives of yore might say. They may not have had office careers, but even Xena, Warrior Princess, would have trouble meeting the exacting standards that housewives of the mid-20th century were expected to achieve. Especially in the Department of Wifely Duties — never mind the kids, the sock-darning and the floor-scrubbing — being a satellite of Planet Husband was a full-time job in itself, similar to that of a celebrity's assistant today.

She's dusted, wiped noses, and bandaged knees. The laundry is folded and the pot roast is warming in the oven. She's ready and waiting with fresh lipstick and smoothed hair. But she hasn't really punched the time clock until the moment her world-weary office gladiator plants one wing-tipped foot through the vestibule.

Then, like an earthbound Tinkerbell, she flits around him in circles till he wants for no more — delivering the highball, the newspaper, the slippers, and the dinner with a smile and eyes overflowing with adoration. Eagerly, she asks questions about his day, benching her own news and musings until further notice.

Disney's animated film version of *Cinderella* was first released in 1950. Even though it was supposed to be for the kids, it also inspired many a young woman to set her pillbox for her very own prince. And like her mother before her, she accepted that finding and keeping royalty at her side required treating him as such.

And, boy howdy, did she have suggestions to help her in her quest! Women's magazines and books of the 1950s and early 1960s offered endless streams of advice on "how to be a good wife," most of which urged women to sublimate their own needs and wants in favor of hââ which by today's mores makes marriage seem more like a police state than bliss:

- **"Accept him at face value — don't try to change him."**

- **"Recognize his superior strength and ability."**

- **"Don't have a lot of preconceived ideas of what you want out of life."**

- **"Revere your husband and honor his right to rule you and your children. Don't stand in the way of his decisions, or his law."**

The medieval, lord-and-serf tone of these tips seems laughable even for the times. Still, the retro housewife's motto was "Never complain, never show strain." No wonder she didn't need Jazzercize classes to keep that wasp-waist trim.

For all her efforts tending to others, she also had a very satisfying secret: her husband, the provider and protector, watched over his nuclear family — but she was its linchpin. Pull her out of the picture, and everything would fall apart!

An Attentive Wife

Unmarried men in the 1950s were often paid less than their married coworkers and had a hard time getting promotions. Employers asserted that equal pay made little sense because a single man's needs were less than that of a family man.

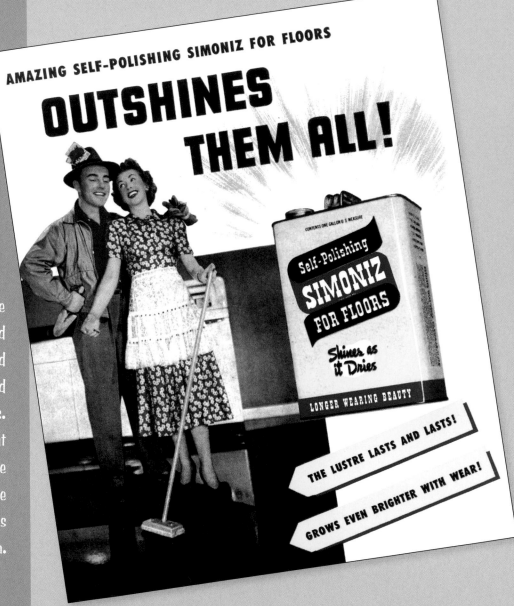

AMAZING SELF-POLISHING SIMONIZ FOR FLOORS

OUTSHINES THEM ALL!

CONTENTS ONE GALLON U.S. MEASURE

Self-Polishing
SIMONIZ
FOR FLOORS

Shines as it Dries

LONGER WEARING BEAUTY

THE LUSTRE LASTS AND LASTS!

GROWS EVEN BRIGHTER WITH WEAR!

There were 1,667,231 marriages in 1950 and 385,144 divorces. Though divorce was rarely considered an acceptable option, the divorce rate hovered around a sizable 23 percent. The new millennium divorce rate is approximately 40 percent.

Pamper Papa!

13

"I HAVE THE NICEST HUSBAND"

In postwar America, marriage was a popular option for young people — especially women. Nearly 25 percent of 18-year-old women were married in 1950 (compared to 4 percent of men), with the number rising to 50 percent among 20-year-olds. Only 32 percent of 25-year-old men remained single that year — double the amount of women the same age.

T.V. moms of the 1950s promoted the standard for housewives across America. June Cleaver of *Leave It To Beaver* and Lucille Ball of *I Love Lucy* were two who went about their daily routines wearing the classic ensemble: stylish high heels, dresses tight at the waist, and pearls. As characters, June portrayed a woman steeped in common sense while Lucy suffered constantly from her tendency toward mischief. For both, things went best when they let her husbands do the big thinking.

cp THIS SEAL certifies that the Gas range carrying it meets all the 22 super-performance standards established by the Gas industry. It stands for the "certified performance" of the range you buy —regardless of the make of the range. Today 24 of America's leading range manufacturers offer CP (certified performance) models. Look for the CP seal when you buy.

17

GAS—

THE __WONDER__ FUEL FOR COOKING

Show your husband (or wife) the new Gas ranges at your Gas Appliance Dealer's or Gas Company. The many exclusive advantages of modern Gas service have been made possible by the Gas utilities of America which, through their laboratories and other agencies, are constantly improving their service to you.

A M E R I C A N   G A S   A S S O C I A T I O N

In 1950, the median age for a first marriage was 20.3 for women and 22.8 for men. By 1998, the median age for first marriages was 25+ for both sexes.

The retro housewife experienced a change in routine once the loved radio show *Guiding Light* was moved to television in 1952. The show had been aired on radio since 1937. (It remains today as the longest running drama in broadcasting history.)

Women in the 1950s were often not
allowed to serve on juries, make contracts
(including mortgages), or establish credit
in their own names.

Adele Davis wrote *Let's Eat Right to Keep Fit* in 1953 and sparked interest in nutrition, health food, and healthy eating. As grocery shoppers and cooks, women were especially intrigued by her findings.

Part-time, home-based businesses gave housewives a chance to earn their own incomes. When Avon launched its "Avon Calling" campaign in 1954, more than 2/3 of Avon employees were women. The company carried more than 500 products and exceeded $55 million in sales annually.

A 1951 Hotpoint automatic dishwasher advertisement directed husbands to "Join the 1,000 men a day who are freeing their wives from dishpan drudgery!" The new machine washed, rinsed, and dried to save wives a whopping hour of work a day.

HOME HOURS ARE HAPPY HOURS WITH THIS WONDERFUL

radio-phonograph...

In the mid-1950s, a "he-man size brandy snifter" catered well to any husband who liked a healthy portion of drink after work. Even nicer on the household budget, this bargain item sold at Macy's for only 49 cents.

The attentive wife could remind her handsome beau of their wedding vows by keeping a wedding ring ashtray handy. This unique gift was a replica of the solid gold ashtray given to Queen Elizabeth and Prince Philip in honor of their 1953 wedding. The ashtray sold in the mid-1950s, had 24-karat gold plating, and came personalized with the couple's names and wedding date for $7.95.

The Kennedy wedding took place on September 13th in 1953 and was one of the biggest events of the year.

27

In addition to Avon and Tupperware, housewives attained degrees of financial independence by selling Shaklee household products. Dr. Forrest C. Shaklee and his two sons founded Shaklee in 1956 and introduced their first product, a biodegradable all-purpose cleaner, in 1960.

In 1945, *How to Win and Hold a Husband* by Kiowa Costonie advised: "Remember that the average man will go as far as you let him go. A man is only as bad as the woman he is with."

The attentive housewife was careful where her family's dollars were spent. That is why she chose Greyhound bus lines for her family travel needs. In 1950, Greyhound boasted homemakers as their biggest clientele.

"I always say <u>nice</u> things about your shirts!"

"Darling, I must warn you — Mother will show you the door!"

Suppose you were visiting your new mother-in-law for the first time. Suppose your husband told you — but wait! It's not what you think.

1 "So you are Bob's Mary! Welcome home, my dear. You children must be starving after that long train ride. Just drop your things anywhere and come right on out in the kitchen. I'll fix you a snack in a jiffy!"

2 "Bob, you idiot! So this refrigerator door is the door your Mother shows me! It's wonderful! All that extra food where you can reach it so easily! Bob, we *must* have a Crosley with the Shelvador* for our new home!"

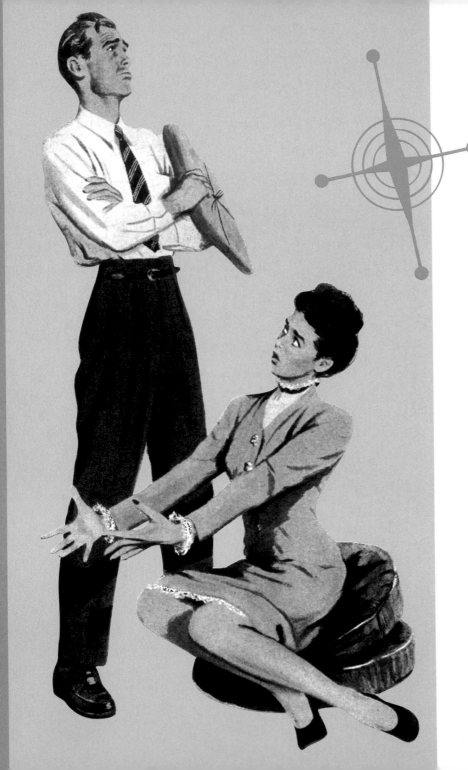

The average life expectancy in the 1950s was age 65 for men and age 71 for women.

Over the course of a decade, the cost of the average family home more than doubled. In 1950, homes sold for $14,500 (compared to $30,000 in 1959).

In some households, a man's wife was the original television remote control. The first electronic version came out in 1950 and was called "Lazy Bones." Zenith Electronics Corporation (known at the time as Zenith Radio Corporation) developed a cable that stretched between the TV and the viewer and operated a motor connected to the tuner. Though convenient, many consumers complained of the device's tacky look and tripping hazard.

As important as being a supportive mate was to every retro housewife, her children's comfort and security were Job One. She dispensed them as regularly as after-school milk and cookies, season after season.

In summer, she gently dotted calamine lotion on mosquito bites and provided daily Kool-Aid breaks. In autumn, she whipped up Halloween costumes and caramel apples for the PTA bake sale. Winter moved to the perpetual rhythm of snowsuits being zipped up and down and congested little chests rubbed with Vicks, and spring came with the annual ritual of dying and hiding Easter eggs.

Images of 1950s TV-idealized super-moms have inextricably merged with memory's reality. Donna Reed is most often touted as the quintessential mother figure of early television. June Cleaver of *Leave It To Beaver*, Harriet Nelson of *Ozzie and Harriet*, and Margaret Anderson of *Father Knows Best* kept their broods famously in order. But the endurance and sphere-of-influence titles should actually go to June Lockhart, who began her career admonishing Timmy not to put his elbows on the table on *Lassie* then donned gravity boots to mete out tenderness and constructive discipline throughout the final frontier on *Lost In Space*.

We knew, even then, that real-life mothers could never fill such mythic proportions. But in 1950, when less than one-third of women worked outside of the home, it was easier to try.

Although the retro housewife spent more time with her children than today's working mothers, she was still anxious about whether she was administering the proper dosages of discipline and affection, praise and criticism. Enter Dr. Benjamin Spock, whose 1946 *Baby and Child Care* sold millions of copies over the next decade (it's now in its seventh printing). Instead of wondering who the heck this man was, telling them how to nurture little Dick and Jane, the moms of America felt grateful for authoritative direction — and perhaps even more, the legitimizing of motherhood as an actual job.

As for punishment, Mom was known to get out the paddle and tap a few light blows on the fanny every now and then. But many baby boomers still flinch involuntarily at the sound of "Wait till your father gets home." Come to think of it, Dad always looked reluctant to spank his children for something they did when he wasn't there.

Mom was an all-knowing, all-seeing, constant presence, a superhero able to heal bruised thumbs and egos in a single bound. There just didn't seem to be too many problems that equal measures of TLC, Ivory soap, and iodine couldn't fix.

And after the bedtime story, she just might have had a few minutes to read another chapter of *Peyton Place* to herself.

Mother Knows Best

35 ▶

Ted Geisel (a.k.a. Dr. Seuss) began his career writing children's books in the 1930s and returned to the profession after producing military training films in Hollywood during WWII. In the 1950s, he produced three of the most cherished children's books of all time: *Horton Hears a Who* (1954), *The Cat in the Hat* (1957), and *How the Grinch Stole Christmas* (1957).

Mothers worried a little less when their children went away to college in the 1950s. The policy of *in loco parentis* authorized colleges to act "in place of the parents" when making student rules. Women had to wear skirts and dresses, sign out when leaving, and return by a designated curfew. In addition, written permission from parents was required if a young woman left for off-campus trips, and any women who married had to drop out. To further suppress social temptations, no members of the opposite sex were allowed to visit dorms.

In 1955, the most popular childrens names included Susan, Linda, Debra/Deborah, Nancy, and Karen for girls and James, David, Robert, John, and Mark for boys.

When kids got sick, Mom was there with popular remedies of the 1950s and from her own childhood. For coughing and congestion, she rubbed Vicks VapoRub on her child's chest and covered the spread with a warm washcloth to release the helpful vapors.

A steamy cup of warm Jell-O or chicken soup kept the fluids going in and out, while a spoonful of cod liver oil once a day delivered important vitamins to boost the immune system.

You've never seen a washer like Frigidaire for getting clothes _really_ clean !

Its Live-Water Action is completely __different__ —designed especially for automatic washing!

"Is your child's future worth a Wurlitzer Piano?" the Rudolph Wurlitzer Company asked parents in the early 1950s. Among other things, the rewarding creativity of piano-playing was said to generate lasting character and personality while providing the joy of music in a child's life. In particular, the piano could teach rowdy sons "poise, perseverance, and self-discipline."

41

In the 1950s, poor nutrition and eating habits were still thought to cause such problems as a child's unruly behavior and mediocre school performance. Ovaltine was a product from Mom's childhood that advertised an easy solution: kids loved the drink's chocolate taste while Mom loved its rich constitution of Iron, Niacin, and Vitamins A, B, C, D, and G.

A trip to grocery stores in the mid-1950s meant more discipline for mothers than in previous decades. The standard U.S. grocery store carried 4,000 items – from new breakfast cereals to soda pops and Jell-O – which far surpassed the basic 870 items in 1928 stores. By the mid-1960s, grocery store stock doubled to 8,000 products.

Back in the 1950s, breakfast started the day right as the most important meal. A week's worth of eggs, toast, bacon, and juice was purchased for under $3 in 1955, satisfying Mom's thrifty and maternal instincts alike.

Ruth Handler joined forces with Mattel to create a new doll in 1959. Barbie, named after Ruth's daughter, had plastic in all the right places to show off an extreme hourglass figure and guide young girls on how to look dainty and pretty.

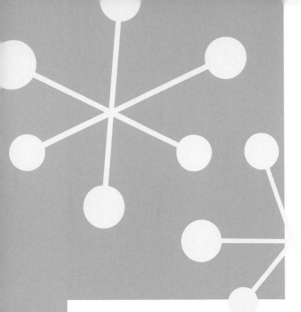

A mother's kiss did well to soothe an injured child, but Band Aid's first decorative bandage secured the deal in 1956. Two years later, the first sheer strip was released.

Disneyland's grand opening on July 17, 1955, was so fresh and new that mothers' heels stuck in the asphalt. The famous cartoon mouse turned into a phenomenon, with the Mickey Mouse Club premiering several months later and 50 million people visiting the park by 1965. The 160-acre wonderland in Anaheim, California, cost $17 million to create and sought to bring families closer together through activities everybody could enjoy.

48

Nitey Nite Sleepers kept kids snug and comfortable in the 1950s, featuring the double sole bootee foot, "I help myself" closings, and sweater cuffs at the sleeves and neck. Most of all, the precious pajamas looked cute, offering the colors Canary, Blueberry, Flamingo, Parakeet, Hummingbird, Tanager, and Robin to outfit boys and girls alike.

In 1954, the U.S. Supreme Court created a stir in the PTA when it ruled that segregation in schools is unconstitutional.

50

Mother Knows Best!

In 1956, one dollar buys only as much food as 41 cents bought in 1939. No wonder Mom pinched those pennies!

Seven-Up invited 1951 families to be "Fresh Up" families, using the refreshing drink to add cheer to home activities or outings. And, no worries, Mom! Seven-Up "is so pure . . . so good . . . so wholesome that even the high chair age can enjoy it often."

Clean rooms and good manners were important to parents in the 1950s, but scientists of the decade struggled to conquer a greater threat. From 1950-1959, Polio swept through the population, killing close to 12,000 children. Jonas Salk began testing a killed virus vaccine in 1954 and gained FDA approval the following year. The breakthrough technology improved lives worldwide.

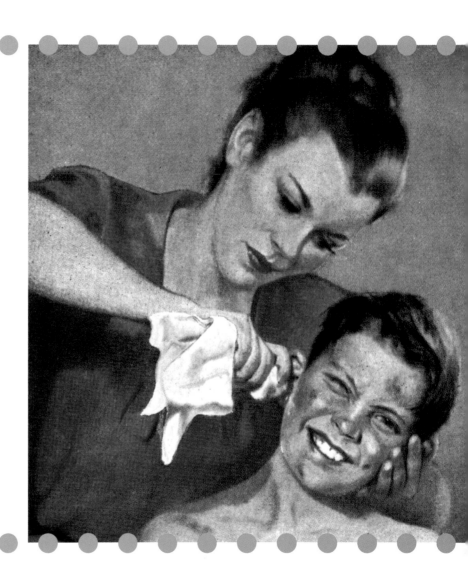

Double your children's play space with Samson Foldaway Furniture! In 1953, a deluxe, five-piece set (folding table and four matching chairs) sold for $49.75, was "a breeze to clean," and came in six mix-n-match colors: Moss, Cocoa, Lime, Peacock, Mist, and Coral.

54

Jif Peanut Butter was introduced in 1956 and answered the call of choosy mothers everywhere!

55

Preparing that bag lunch got easier in 1950 when Kraft foods introduced pre-sliced cheeses to the supermarket.

In 1955, James Dean's movie *Rebel Without a Cause* took a controversial step when it focused on a rarely discussed but common sentiment of alienation and disenchantment among American teenagers.

f the retro housewife's home was a spiritual haven, the kitchen was her most sacred space. And Betty Crocker was its saint.

Betty was a marketing tool created to sell flour. Yet she came to represent so much more: the embodiment of a woman who provides her family with three square meals a day. From Schenectady to San Diego, her disciples were legionary, enthusiastically sifting flour, basting roasts, and rolling out strips of latticed dough to top their signature cherry pies.

Cooking from scratch was not a pastime to be dabbled with on weekends and holidays. It was an everyday necessity.

During the rationing days of World War II, frugal housewives skimped on meat and sugar, saving the excess fat from their cooking to donate to explosives manufacturers. By the early 1950s, optimism and incomes prospered, and the world was her smorgasbord — or at least, the gleaming new supermarket down the road was.

She spent her mornings shopping, her afternoons baking and listening to the *Kitchen Klub*, a syndicated radio program broadcast form New York to Denver. She didn't have the microwave ovens or food processors of today to help her turn out five-star meals. Such advances in technology as the Frigidaire icebox and Hamilton Beach mixer — not to mention Jell-O, Tupperware, and the lightweight casserole dishes she could buy at the giant new supermarket —afforded all the exciting innovation she could imagine. But all that was nothing compared to a 1954 invention debuted by Swanson & Sons — the TV dinner.

One portion each of meat, starch, and that all-important vegetable, whisked from oven to table in one easy step — removing the aluminum-foil wrapper. This was women's liberation retro housewife style — but only in emergencies, of course!

Most housewives spent at least three hours a day in the kitchen, preparing food, doing dishes, and cleaning. One of the keys to the popularity of the ranch-style home was its centralized, open kitchen, which allowed Mom to feel less like a scullery maid and more like a ship's captain at the helm.

The kitchen even took on political significance during the Cold War. If there was any doubt of this room's importance to the American dream, it was laid to rest after the "kitchen debate" between Richard Nixon, then vice-president of the United States, and Soviet leader Nikita Khrushchev in 1959. The first-ever American exhibit opened in Moscow, featuring a model of a kitchen packed with technologically advanced appliances that was said to represent the "typical American home." While standing in that kitchen in front of news cameras, the two men engaged in a remarkably heated argument about whether capitalism or communism would eventually rule the world. Why this room? No one knows for sure, but it seems likely that such an altar to American economic success would spark emotion on both sides.

Today's kitchen has evolved even further as the heart of the family home, leaving dining rooms to collect dust until company comes. At many a successful party, the most crowded room is the kitchen because it means home, warmth, food — and Mom.

The Way to the Heart

Simplify recipe and cookbook storage in your 1950s kitchen! A wise wife purchased The American Home Menu Maker, which featured 1,000 illustrated 3 x 5-inch cards stored in a compact recipe box. Available through mail order, it cost an economical $2.50.

The housewife who wanted to earn extra points with her hard-working husband cooked up a nice T-Bone steak for a cost of 95 cents per pound in 1954.

Fresh from the freezer, Clarence Birdseye marketed the first frozen version of an important staple in 1952: green peas. That same year, Mrs. Paul's completes the mealtime ensemble with the introduction of frozen fish sticks.

NOW!

As early as 1947, Hotpoint developed a fast-cooking electronic oven to meet rising demands for kitchen efficiency. The oven heated pre-cooked foods in approximately one minute and was ultimately marketed to the fast food industry.

62

Swanson preceded its breakthrough TV dinner with the introduction of frozen pot pies in 1951. The easy dinners came in beef, chicken, and turkey and boasted 400 million sales in 1958 alone.

The 1950s kept options open for service pieces in the kitchen and on the table. Dow plastics created all kinds of colorful accessories, from salt and pepper shakers to water jugs and butter dishes, while deLux Melmac provided heavier, more sturdy (dishwasher friendly) dinnerware. Who can forget Colorama's aluminum cups, pitchers, and plates? Their colors were "scientifically fused into the metal for everlasting brilliance."

Small electric appliances did wonders for cooking. Oster, General Electric, Sunbeam, and Hamilton Beach led the way with coffeemakers, hand-held mixers, toasters, skillets, can openers, waffle irons, and more! In 1956, GE advertised a $16.95 Speed Kettle that boiled water quickly and automatically shut-off.

64

Glass cookware brought color, durability, and storage options to the 1950s kitchen, with red, blue, green, yellow, turquoise, and pink balancing clear glass choices. Pyrex was a common brand, in addition to Anchorglass, offering such items as mixing bowls, saucepans, oven and refrigerator sets, covered casserole dishes, and even matching dinnerware.

65

Birdseye eliminated potato scrubbing, peeling, and cutting in 1955 when it premiered frozen Potato Patties. Housewives simply fried the patties on both sides until they were cooked through and evenly browned.

Trading stamps offered a smart way to stretch the 1950s household budget. Every supermarket and gas station visit generated brand-name stamps, with King Korn, Top Value, Plaid, and S&H Green Stamps being the most popular. After enough were pasted in the saver's book, the stamps could be redeemed for household goods and small appliances.

Have friends stopping over or an unexpected guest? Nobody doesn't like this solution! The Sara Lee Baked Goods Company was founded in 1949 and developed a freezing technique that allowed perishable products, like their famous "New York Cheesecake," to be shipped throughout the country.

68

Though housewives of yesteryear never admitted it, they secretly rejoiced when Ray Kroc started the McDonald's Corporation in 1955. Founded on the new fast food notion, opening day sales of $366.12 indicated America was ready to embrace its food on the fly.

The one billionth can of Spam sold in 1959.

Cooks in 1955 also witnessed the debut of Instant Oatmeal by the Quaker Oats Company, Del Monte Stewed Tomatoes (based on the recipe of an employee's mother), and Pineapple Grapefruit Juice.

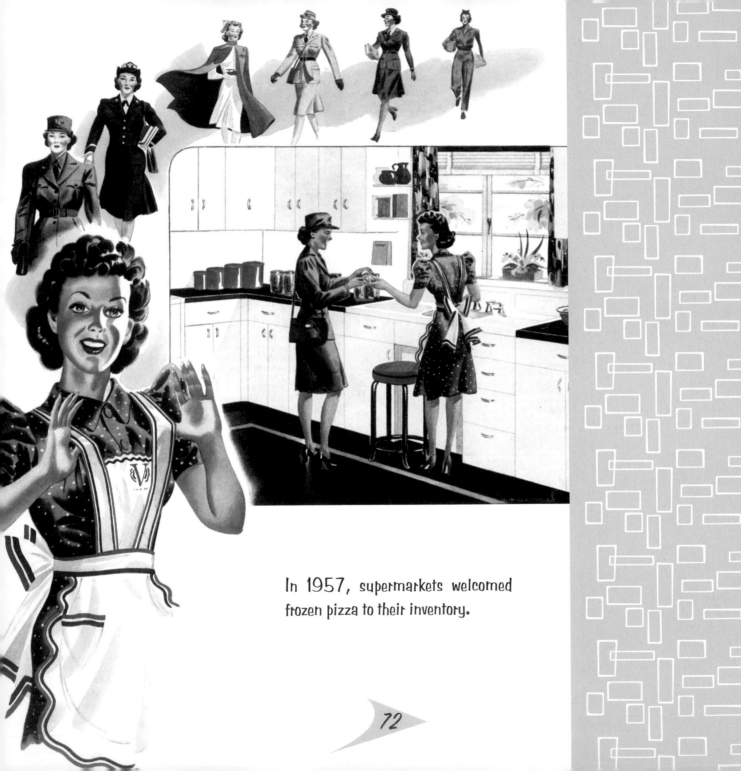

In 1957, supermarkets welcomed frozen pizza to their inventory.

Diner's Club issued the first credit card in 1951 to 200 customers for use in 27 New York restaurants. Card holders could only use the card for meal payments.

Never before such a kitchen  for cooking!

Mom's life got easier in 1954 when Gerald Thomas of Swanson & Sons invented the first TV dinner. A surplus of Thanksgiving turkeys inspired him to create a frozen meal simply prepared from oven to table. The first dinner included cornbread dressing and gravy, sweet potatoes, and buttered peas served in a disposable aluminum tray.

How does a busy mother keep up with PTA meetings, all her jobs at home, and the daily task of feeding the family? The Magic Chef has the answer! This gas oven and range advertised in 1954 as being "so automatic you can load it and leave it and come back to a perfectly cooked dinner hours later."

Fred Mennen refined a hull-free yellow corn to create Jiffy Pop popcorn, introducing the product to the public in 1959. Though it took him five years to perfect the hybrid corn, Jiffy Pop achieved national distribution by 1960.

During the 1961 holiday season, the Kennedy Company advertised a Musical Christmas Apron to add an extra bit of holiday cheer to the housewife's wardrobe. The decorative accessory came fully equipped with ribbons, bells, and the cook's name embroidered on the front with glow-in-the-dark thread.

they're *femineered* !

Mom knew how a piping-hot cup of coffee got Dad started before going off to work in the morning. In 1955, one pound of coffee cost approximately 93 cents a pound, which was 20 cents more per pound than the cost of his favorite sirloin chops.

79

In the heyday of the housewife, the only man doing any tidying up around the homestead was the completely fictitious Mr. Clean. And even *he* wasn't around in the early days. Hiring outside help to do your dusting and laundry was unheard of, so that left all the housework to Mama — a situation many modern women might insist has changed little.

Back then, cleaning products required much more human effort to make them work. As a result, the housewife ended up burning three times the calories that her modern counterparts do. Perhaps it's more than nostalgia fueling the trend in retro cleaners such as Mrs. Meyer's brand and others found at stores like Restoration Hardware.

In the 1940s, she relied almost solely on elbow grease to keep grime from invading and occupying her nest. The family home of the Eisenhower era was so bright; every surface reflected sanitized satisfaction. At least, that's how advertisers envisioned the new suburban utopia.

Housecleaning was drudgery raised to an art form. She tucked perfect hospital corners under the mattress, waxed the linoleum on hand and knee, brushed dirt on the front steps into her Rubbermaid dust pan, polished the Sunbeam Mixmaster to a high gloss, and added ample splashes of Clorox to get those linens whiter than white (and let's not forget she washed and re-used cloth diapers again and again).

The bronze baby shoes and Hummel figurines received a daily buffing (as Mom daydreamed about being Jane Wyman in *Magnificent Obsession*). The wood was blond, the lampshades fiberglass, the countertops Formica, the toaster gleaming chrome accented with bakelite — all were ready to impress drop-in visitors, from the neighbors to the man selling Fuller brushes or encyclopedias door-to-door.

Automation and electricity were the domestic engineer's best friends, most beloved when powering such appliances as the iron and the vacuum cleaner. The Electrolux vacuum featured a disposable bag that ejected when full — years before the Jetsons arrived on the scene.

With the leisure time made possible by these time-saving devices, the 1950s home also became a neighborhood gathering spot, where mothers could get their girl time in before those demanding Dads came home, maybe play a few hands of bridge, or throw a Tupperware party while the kids romped in the backyard.

A growing number of books on keeping the modern house have been published over the past several years. All of them contain enough tried-and-true tips, handed down from retro housewives, to fill a laundry basket.

Necessity, as the adage goes, is the *mother* of invention — not the father. Is it any surprise that a woman perfected the dishwasher?

A Home That Sparkles

81

In 1960, Proctor and Gamble released their first fabric softener, Downy.

A May 1953 *House Beautiful* article instructs housekeepers to relax when it comes to new technology and streamlined work. Modern dryers, for example, were designed with a "Lo-Heat-Hi-Breeze" concept intended to dry at temperatures low enough for delicates. The article also addresses weight-lifting phobias with its introduction of the new, 16-pound Apex vacuum on wheels.

82

By the start of 1950, companies like Bendix, GE, and Hoover developed affordable appliances that reduced a housewife's work time by half. In 1949, she could own a Bendix tumble-action washing maching, a Bendix dryer with new "Suntronic Lamp" (dried clothes using ultraviolet rays), and a Bendix heavy-duty ironer for a $47.50 down payment.

"Have a 'Company-Clean' home every day . . . in minutes!" with the 1953 Regina Electrikbroom. For only $39.95, the machine did the work of an upholstery brush, dust mop, and carpet sweeper with no cumbersome attachments or bags. It "saves on Mother's strength and health [and] doctors approve its lightness."

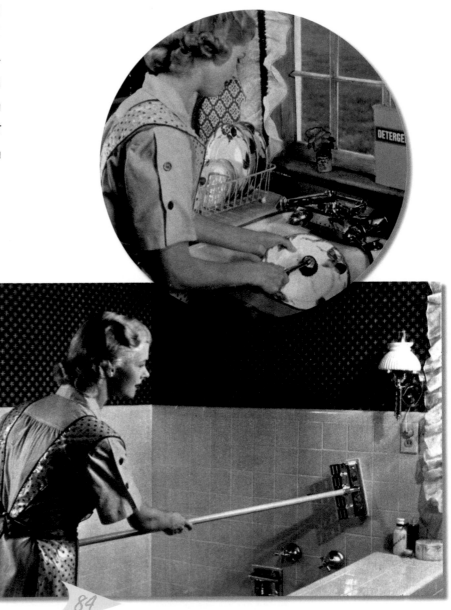

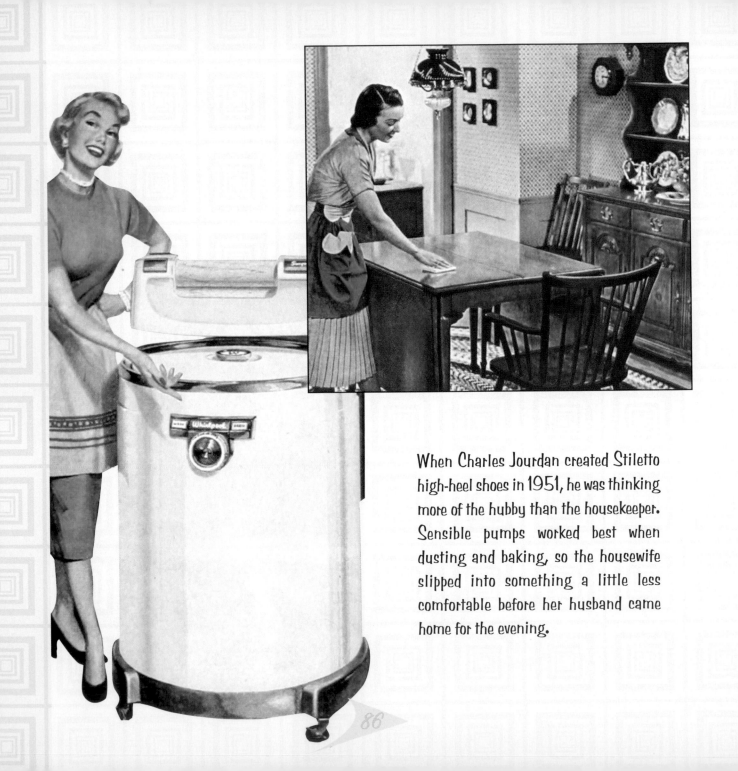

When Charles Jourdan created Stiletto high-heel shoes in 1951, he was thinking more of the hubby than the housekeeper. Sensible pumps worked best when dusting and baking, so the housewife slipped into something a little less comfortable before her husband came home for the evening.

Tide hit the consumer test markets in October 1946 and received an immediate response. Advertised as the world's first heavy-duty detergent, it outsold all other brands in a week's time and grew so popular stores had to limit the quantity each customer could buy. In Tide's first 21 years on the market, its formula was improved 22 times.

Dixie Cups did a lot to free up Mom's time cleaning dishes. In 1951, a "smart, new crystal-clear home dispenser" went on sale and could be mounted in a number of convenient locations.

Use the "window test" to see how your laundry detergent compares to Cheer. "In that honest, natural light, you'll see the bright, new whiteness Cheer gives your wash." In 1955, Cheer was preferred by 8 out of 10 women with agitator washing machines.

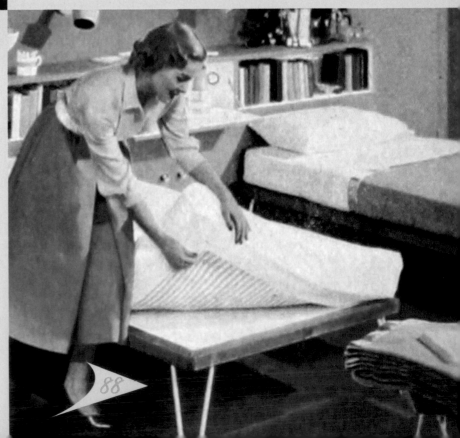

The Electrolux model LXI sold from 1952 to 1955 and featured one of the first disposable paper bags. When full, the vacuum shut down, its front cover opened, and the bag ejected out — automatically!

89

Having a home with modern appliances also required creative storage to maintain daily efficiency and productivity. A 1951 issue of *Companion* magazine suggested hiding large appliances behind decorative curtains and saving space by building shelves that stowaway in the walls and slide out for instant work stations.

IT'S FUN!

TO CLEAN

THIS MODERN WAY!

Refrigerators received extreme makeovers in 1958, including the introduction of frost-free freezers, automatic icemakers, forced air refrigeration, and condenser coils moved to the bottom from the back. Clothes dryers also evolved that year, featuring dryness controls, programmed cycles, and automatic dispensers for bleach and fabric softeners.

See if it doesn't **CLEAN FASTER. EASIER** than any other cleanser you've ever used!

In 1953, Saran Wrap® film revolutionized household food storage as the first cling wrap in the consumer market. Dow Chemical Company introduced the product, which is marketed in the new millennium by S. C. Johnson.

General Electric invented the nifty 2-door refrigerator/freezer combination in 1947, with the freezer maintaining temperatures of 10 degrees F while the fridge kept foods cool at 38 degrees F. Theoretically, the freezer never needed defrosting because it did not have a chance to infringe on refrigerator space.

Handy inventions of the 1950s included a combination freezer/table featuring a table top that mounted to a freezer. Inside, the freezer maintained 5 1/2 cubic feet of storage with two drawers designed for easy access to oddly shaped items.

Home laundry innovations in 1953 introduced the combination washer/dryer and more compact, 24-inch washers and dryers.

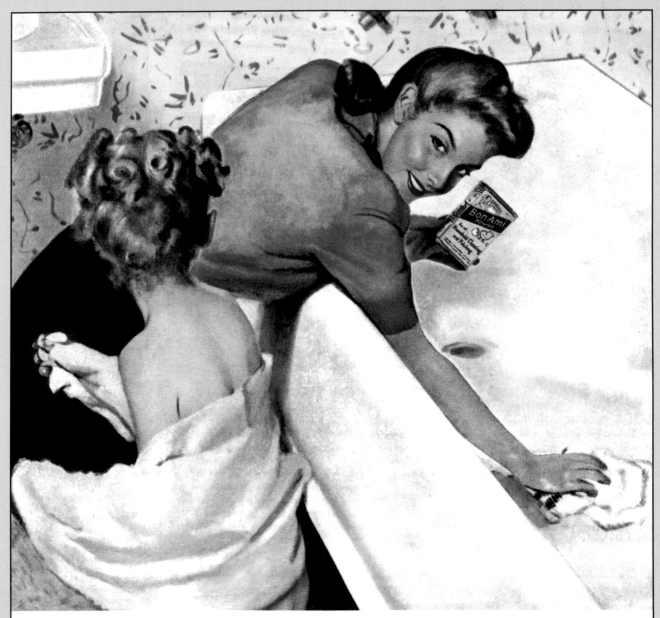

"In a minute the tub will be as shiny as <u>you</u>, darling!"

Fifty cents and a Spic and Span box top bought three mail order Food-Saver bags in the late 1940s. Before Ziploc baggies and Tupperware, these storage bags were the best at keeping veggies fresh.

Cover a variety of household needs with a multi-tasking product! In the 1940s and 1950s, the Lever Brothers Company produced Rinso (with Solium), which supposedly had "3 times the whiter washing action of any other soap" AND doubled as a dishwashing detergent. Now, that's efficient!

In 1955, Colgate-Palmolive made home a little sweeter with its release of the first air freshener, packaged in a convenient 5 1/2-ounce aerosol can.

For a final touch to the living room, Mom put out a *TV Guide* on the coffee table to advertise her household's modern mindset. The first *TV Guide* was published in 1953 and generated 1.5 million copies in its first printing.

Of all the specialty products made
for automatic washers in 1956,
Dash laundry detergent was said
to get clothes the cleanest!

The middle class suburban woman ran her home on a tight budget. Just because the family income was expanding didn't mean she could toss frugality out with the dishwater. She was financially dependent on her husband, and there was no better way to ensure a steady stream of cash than to demonstrate her ability to spend as little as possible.

Going out to dinner was a special treat reserved for wedding anniversaries. She saved her Green Stamps and clipped ten-cent coupons. She sewed most of her family's clothes, did her own painting and repairs, and waited for deals on Hawaiian bark cloth at the fabric store when she wanted to update her slipcovers. The only hobby she had time for was knitting. There was no shame in hand-me-downs, especially nursery furniture and children's clothing. Keeping up with Joneses was important but not more important than staying out of debt. She replaced the furniture when it became threadbare or broken down and not before.

Camelback sofas topped with doilies gave way to the kidney-shaped coffee tables, Danish-modern upholstery protected with Scotchgard, and kitschy ceramics of the Atomic Age. Still, her woman's touch graced every room. Hand-embroidered dish towels hung neatly on racks in the kitchen, the aromas of lavender and lilac wafted up from the linens, rosebushes lined the patio, and lace-edged dust ruffles adorned her little bobby-soxers' beds.

Vacuuming may not have been performed in heels and pearls quite as often in real life as it was in the pages of magazines. But the retro housewife was still urged as never before to keep her own appearance impeccable — now that she had attracted her man, she'd best figure out how to keep him.

In the 1930s, newspaper and magazine ads targeted women by focusing on clothing and grooming aids. By the 1950s, along with the rise of Kraft and Procter & Gamble, food and household products had taken over the no. 1 spot. No matter the product, however, the model promoting it looked fabulous. As consumerism increased, so did the value of an attractive image.

Visits from the Avon Lady came in handy in an age when being seen retrieving the mail without freshly applied lipstick was a fashion faux pas. It was hard to find the time, but weekly appointments at the beauty parlor for a wash-and-set were a must.

One ad campaign for brassieres, risqué for the 1950s, featured women from the waist up wearing only a bra, with the caption: "I dreamed I sang a duet at the Met in my Maidenform." Even if she was only picking up Johnny from baseball practice, the retro housewife was supposed to feel glamorous at all times.

Every now and then, she felt just a little bit cross about working as hard as her husband and having to look perpetually perfect while doing it. Then he walked in the door, and all was sunshine once more.

That Feminine Touch

Plasti-Chrome shelving paper and edging was a signature marking of 1950s kitchen decor. With patterns like Bridal Roses, Pond Lilies, and Apple Cluster, every shelf was sure to have a beautifully ruffled edge.

Freshening her makeup before hubby came home was a kind way for a wife to greet her man after a long day. Maybelline, Max Factor, and Ponds were big brand names in the 1950s, competing with new face powders, lipsticks, and eye treatments. The mascara wand also eliminated all kinds of application troubles with its invention in 1958.

longer lasting...it's genuine lacquer

Like the fabulous lacquers of old, new Chen Yu is *made* to last longer. Faster drying, harder setting, extra brilliant...it's *genuine* lacquer. Extra safe, too. 12 beautiful new fashion-cued colors...lighter, brighter, fashion smarter, in Chen Yu's exclusive new finger-rest container for quicker, easier, cleaner application.

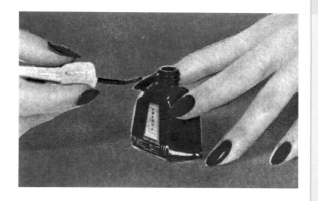

107

Lady Esther Lipcolors kept up with women's busy lifestyles by creating one of the first long-lasting lipsticks in the early 1950s. Colors ranged from Bridal Pink to Crimson Bronze and sold for one dollar each.

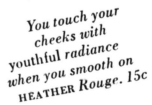

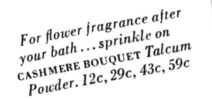

For flower fragrance after your bath...sprinkle on CASHMERE BOUQUET Talcum Powder. 12c, 29c, 43c, 59c

You touch your cheeks with youthful radiance when you smooth on HEATHER Rouge. 15c

After WWII, Revlon started a seasonal revolution with bi-annual nail enamel and lipstick promotions. Using television sponsorship to push their lines, business boomed with new colors and sales. A sampler box of nail polish, lipstick, and lip liner cost $1.60 plus tax in one of their 1950s ads.

Protect Summer daintiness with new FRESH *Deodorant...softer, creamier than ever!*
12c, 27c, 43c, 63c

Colors that cling to your lips...won't eat off or kiss off! HAZEL BISHOP *Lipstick, 59c Jumbo swivel case, 1.10*

A housewife who loves cuddly kittens could purchase a Siamese cat TV light in 1956 for $7.95. The porcelain cats had "china blue" eyes, which sent a light glow out into the room and were lovely even when turned off.

Ever conscious of climate in the home, Mom was glad when the dehumidifier was introduced for home use in 1952.

BE SURE YOU GET
EVERYTHING
A MODERN
BLIND
SHOULD
HAVE!

Arthur Godfrey got in on the act of selling fiberglass curtains in 1953. The new material required no ironing, came ruffled, tailored, or in tiers, was guaranteed for five years, and could hang dry in seven minutes. As he said, "Beautiful, and they save you work and money too!"

The first oral contraceptives were developed in 1954 but were not available to the public until the early 1960s. Laced with traces of early feminism, the drug threatened the housewife tradition. Margaret Sanger, who advocated women's rights and helped to fund the pill's development, said: "No woman can call herself free until she can choose consciously whether she will or will not be a mother."

In 1954, Matico Mastic Tile was "the brightest, gayest flooring idea in years . . . perfect for your kind of living." This economically friendly flooring alternative was easy to clean, easy to install, and available in ten confetti color combinations.

"Who's my decorator? Me—with the help of the Singer Sewing Center!"

Cannon made all kinds of color combinations and bathroom upgrades possible with its 1954 Carefree Color line. The campaign utilized eighteen colors and three different fabrics to customize any bathroom with matching bath towels, washcloths, and hand towels. Prices ranged from 79 cents to $3.50.

"Give your old nylons a cat's lease on life with these easy tricks." The October 1955 issue of *Everywoman's* magazine printed 9 easy tips for reusing old nylons, including making balls for children, using them as shoe protectors, creating woven table mats, and handy hairbrush slipcovers.

Hand-painted kitchen canisters and matching accessories were popular in the 1950s and made a woman's kitchen her own. Ransburg Originals offered 19-piece sets in an array of floral patterns for $7. The bargain set featured five canisters in descending sizes, a cake cover, a bread box, a coupon holder, and a trash can.

Wall-Tex and Kimberly-Clark Wallpapers brought a designer touch to the 1950s with a vast variety of colors, textures, and patterns. The 1954 Fall line of Kimberly-Clark advertised looks like Grass Cloth, Mountain Laurel, Strawberry Farm, Herbs, Chintz, and Homespun patterns. With tight budgets in mind, the designs came in jumbo, 9-foot rolls for $1.79 each.

In 1950, Lawrence Gelb introduced one-step hair coloring to America with Miss Clairol Hair Color Bath. He founded Clairol in 1932 using the formula of a Paris hair color product with the same name. Being a blonde bombshell was one step closer to possible, and women flocked to salons to get tinted.

Functional and beautiful too, mail order items offered a variety of decorating options. In 1953, the creative homemaker could buy a wood magazine show case for $17.50, Velon furniture protectors (in a variety of sizes) starting at $3.95, a copper, custom-made waste basket with the family dog's breed and name for $15.00, or a colorful Tankette 3-piece toilet set for $3.98. One's imagination was the only limiting factor!

"I spent less than $50 to re-do this love-of-a-LIVING ROOM!"

121

tuned to traditional?

If a room needed some color or framing, borders provided a simple touch of style. Monarch Electric, makers of the Roaster Range Oven, sold kitchen borders in the 1950s for 30 cents per 12-foot roll. Often featuring images of daily household duties, the border attached easily to the wall with a quick dip in water.

or merrily modern?

Who could avoid looking stylish in dress styles with names like "sheath" and "sack"? When the day's work was done, the 1950s Mom left the house wearing clean, neat fashions worthy of any French magazine. Higher heels or Stilettos, skirts with lower hemlines, and narrow, pinched waists completed the evening look.

How much of **YOU** is in your home?

123

Before pop culture, there was domestic culture. An American woman's life revolved almost exclusively around her home and family. Then the wheels of social evolution rolled right over that standard role and on to broader horizons.

When you think about it, housewives were poised for outside careers all along. In the home, they had all the necessary skills to launch a successful business — managing schedules, balancing budgets, hosting dinner parties for hubby's boss, and devising creative, spontaneous solutions to daily problems.

Current books and magazines on how to be a domestic goddess aren't bestsellers because the clock is turning back. They're popular because

women do want to have it all. In other words, they want the freedom, power, and independence they have now, plus the security, extra time with children, and uncomplicated lives enjoyed by their forebears: those resourceful, resplendent, and now "retro" housewives.

More than ever, there is comfort in focusing on the inner sanctum rather than the uncertain world outside. The idea of a real 40-hour work week and whole families eating dinner together at the same time is impossibly romantic. Looking back, the life of a 1950s housewife appears idyllic to harried working people. Do the dishes, bake a pie, then polish the coffee table until you can see your face in it. What luxury!

Nostalgia has never been so popular, as we can see from baby boomers' enthusiasm for buying remakes of toys and cookie jars from their childhood days. But the retro housewife is no mass-reproduced tchotchke. She's a warm and fuzzy memory — a memory that, for all its idealistic rose-tinting, is based on something very real: the love and sense of security she radiated with an energy that seemed, well, practically atomic.

Oh my, but this has been fun. You may be all grown up, but Mom still wants to know: Did you take your vitamins? Are you wearing clean underwear? If not — just wait till your father gets home.